JUST ADD COLOR

MID-CENTURY MODERN PATTERNS

30 ORIGINAL ILLUSTRATIONS
TO COLOR, CUSTOMIZE, AND HANG

ARTWORK BY JENN SKI

Rockport Publishers
100 Cummings Center, Suite 406L
Beverly, MA 01915

rockpub.com • rockpaperink.com

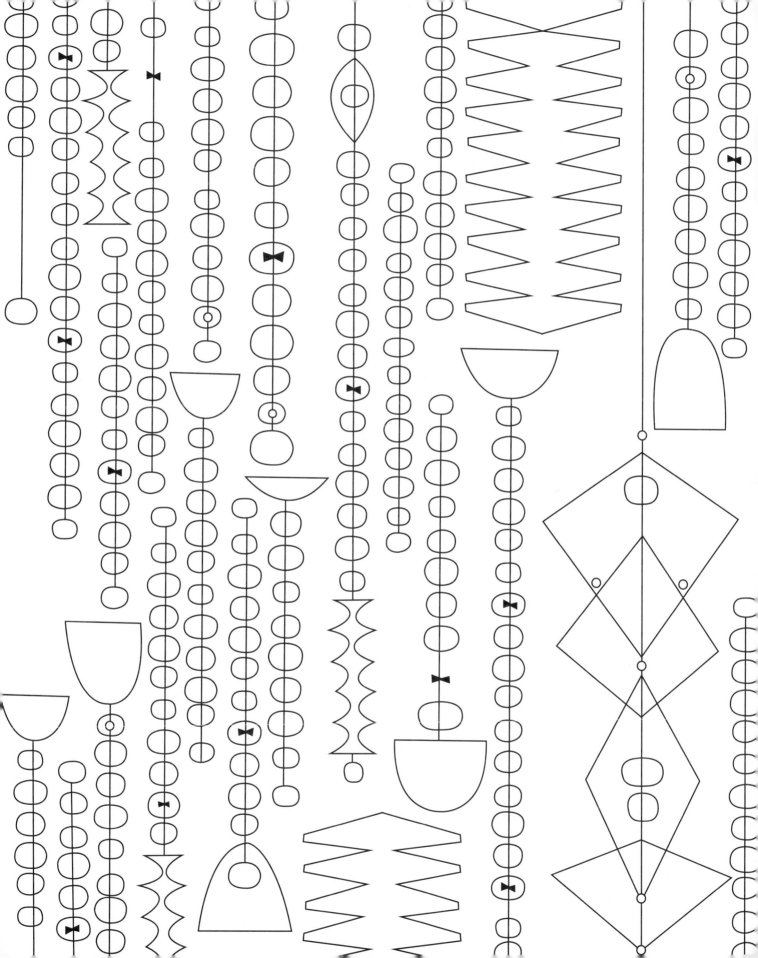

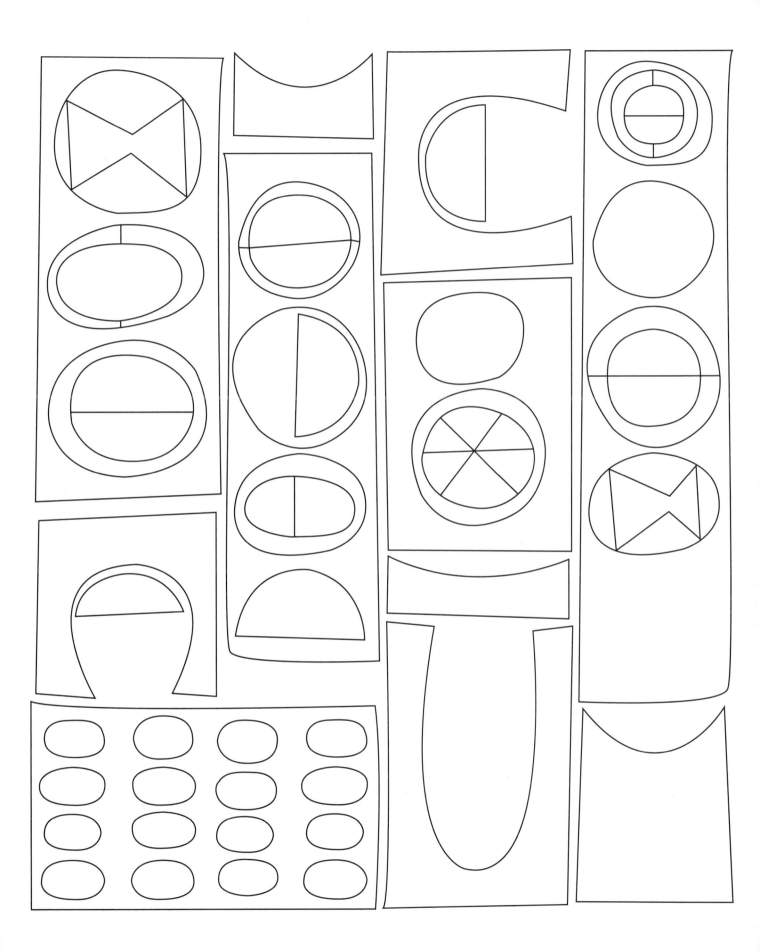

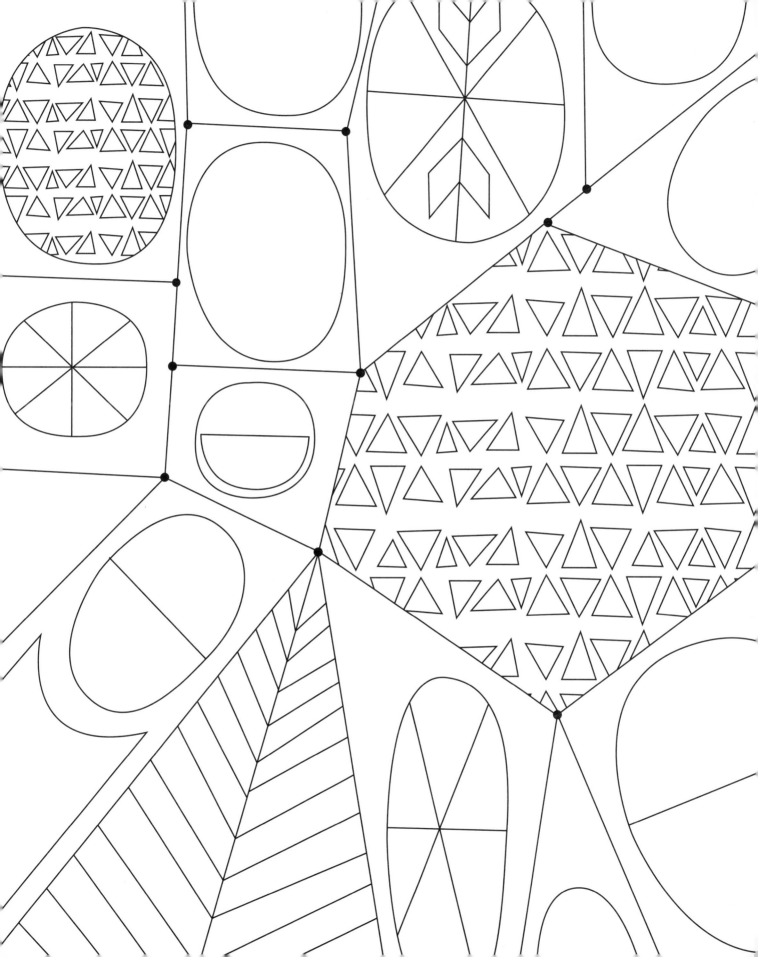

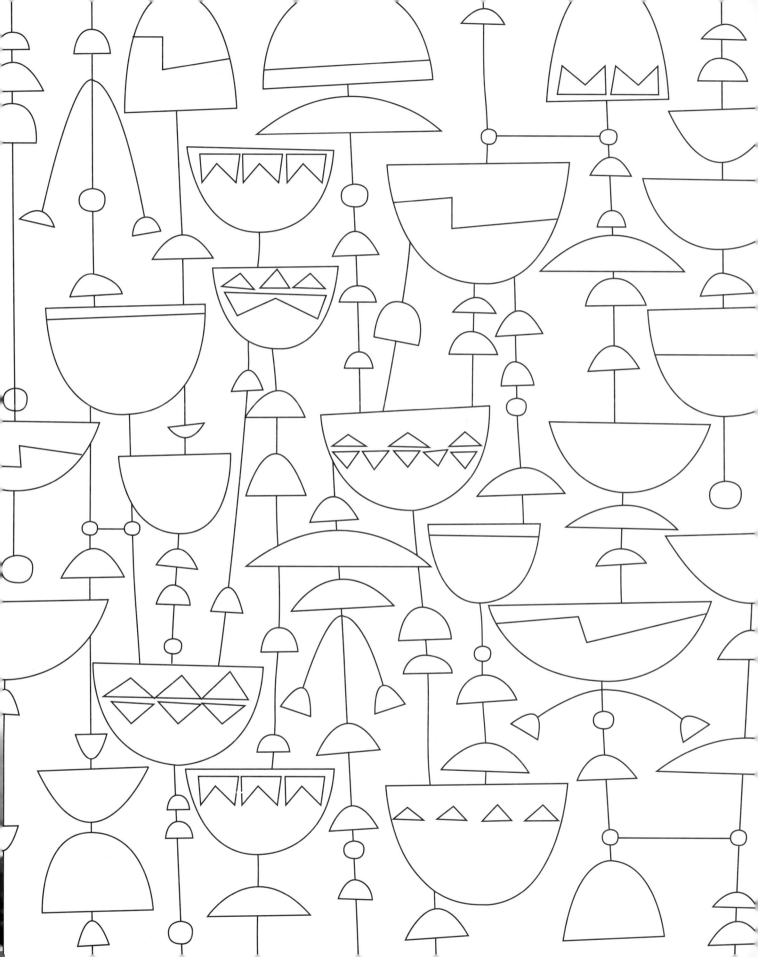

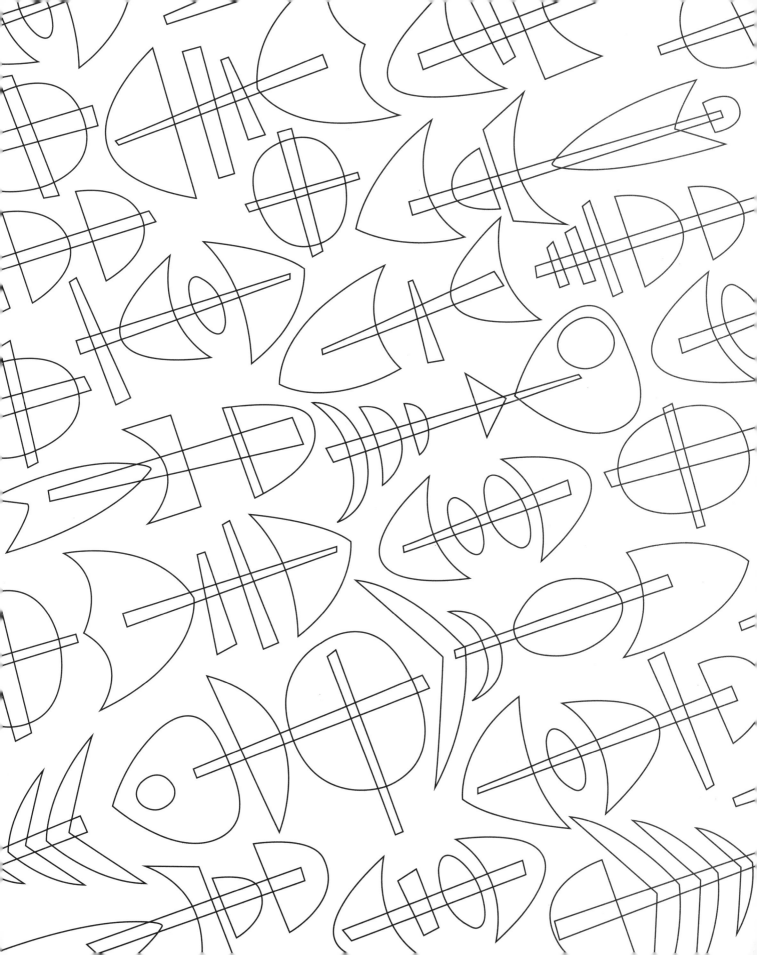

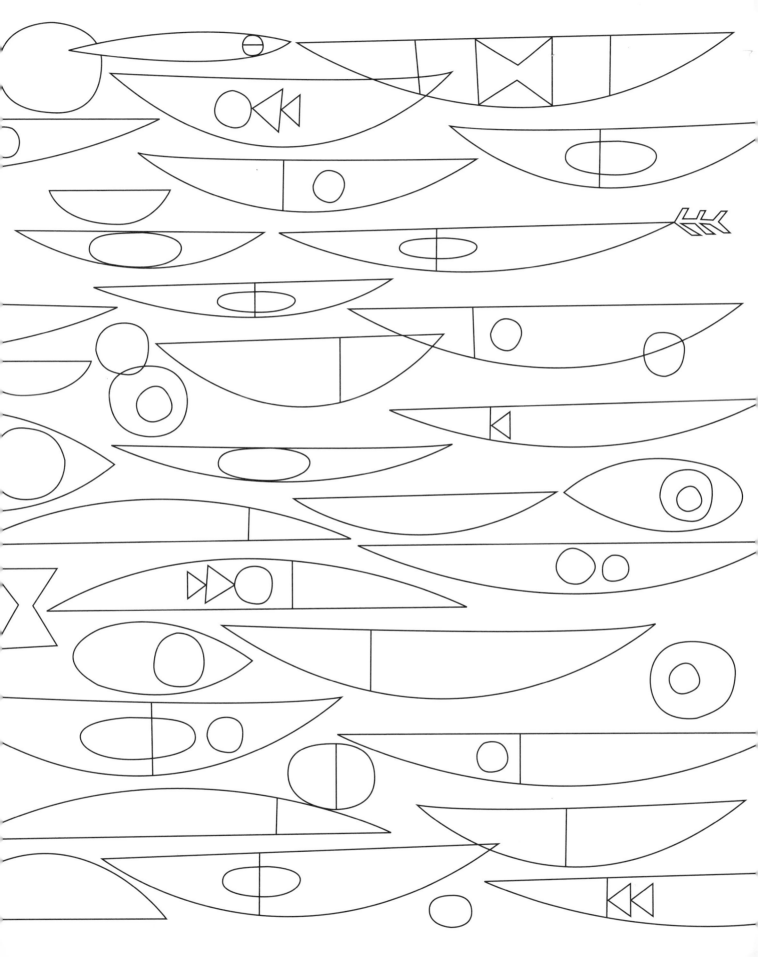

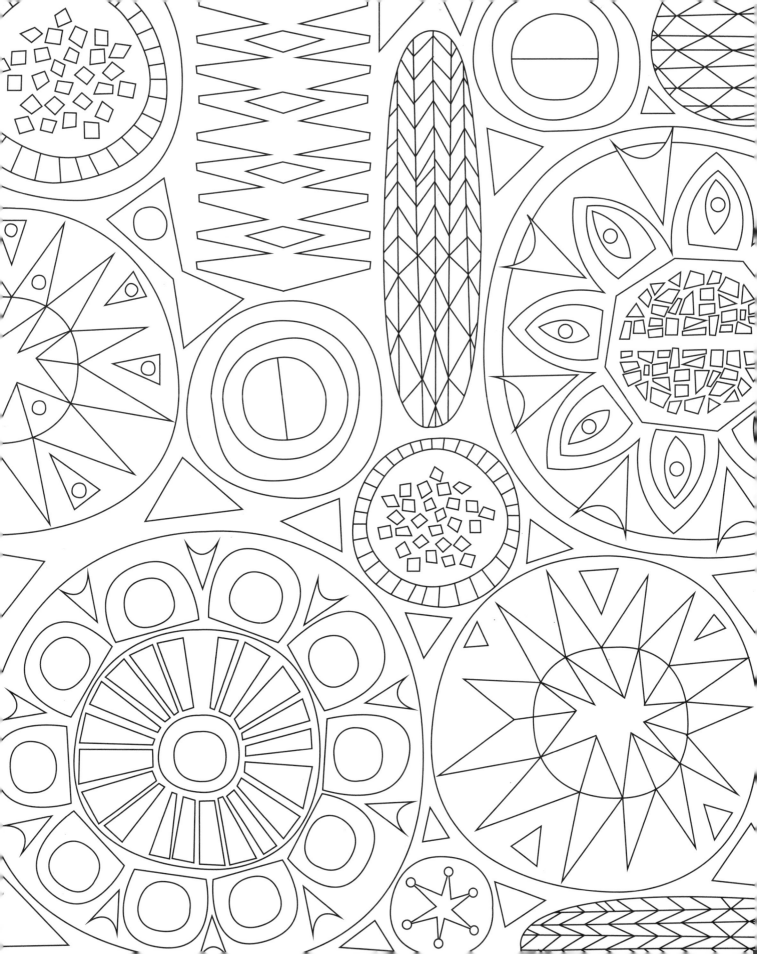

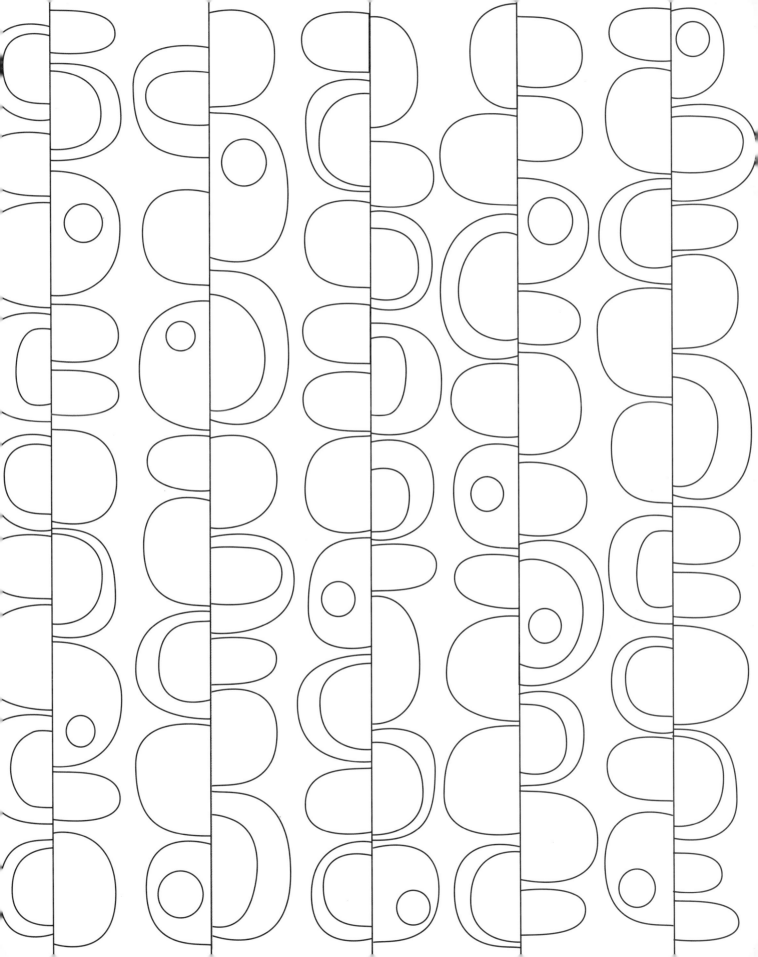

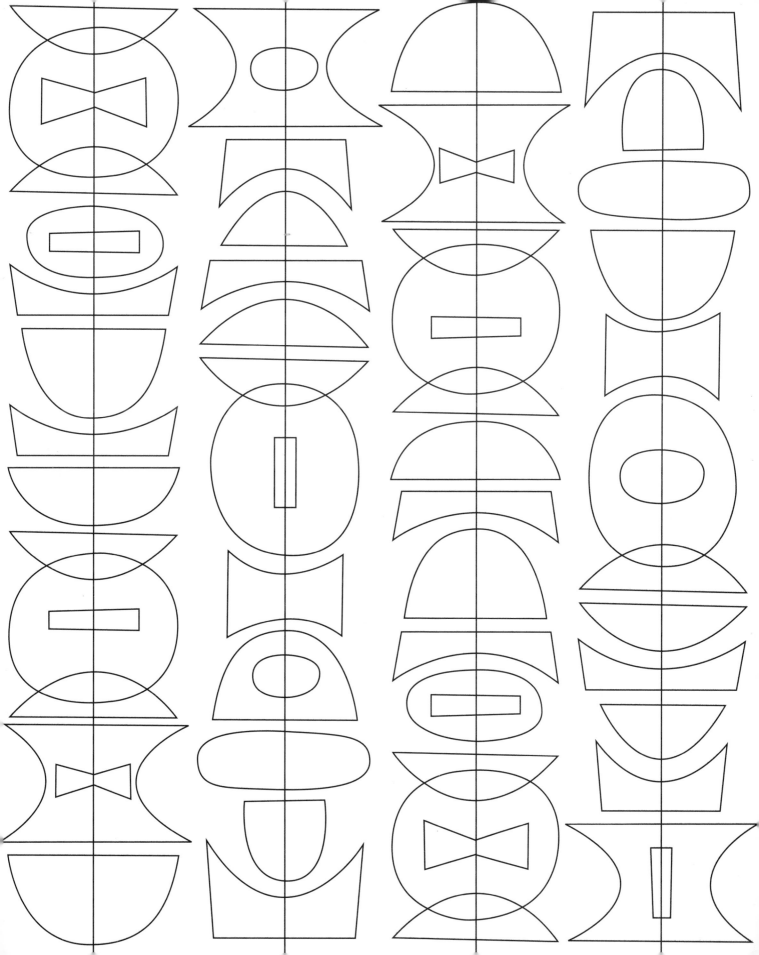

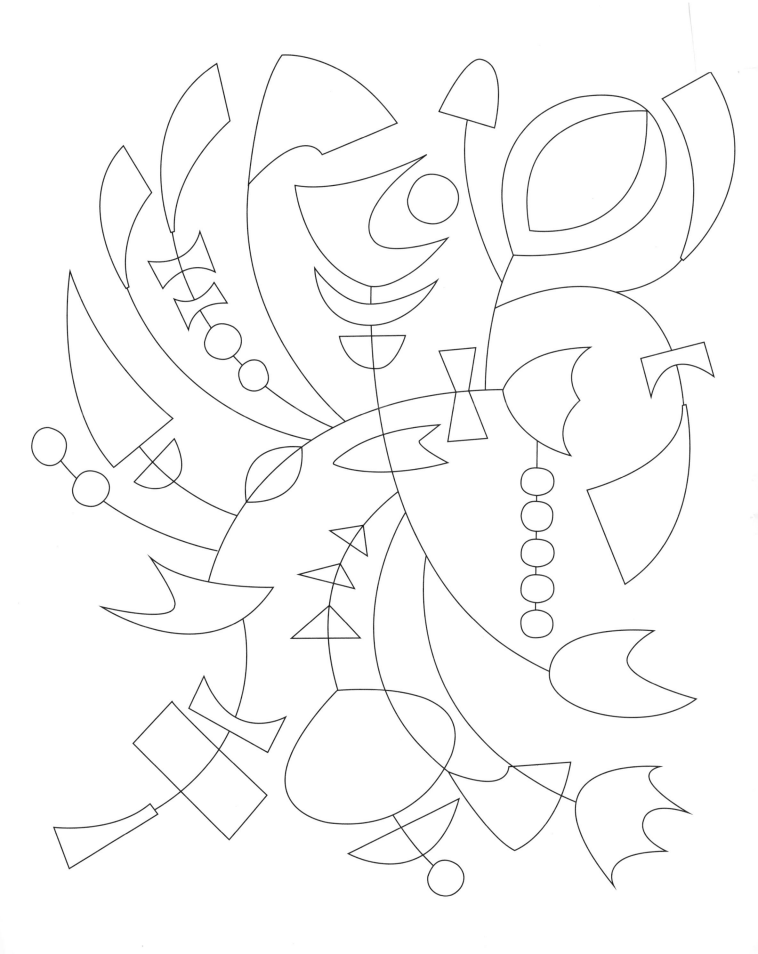

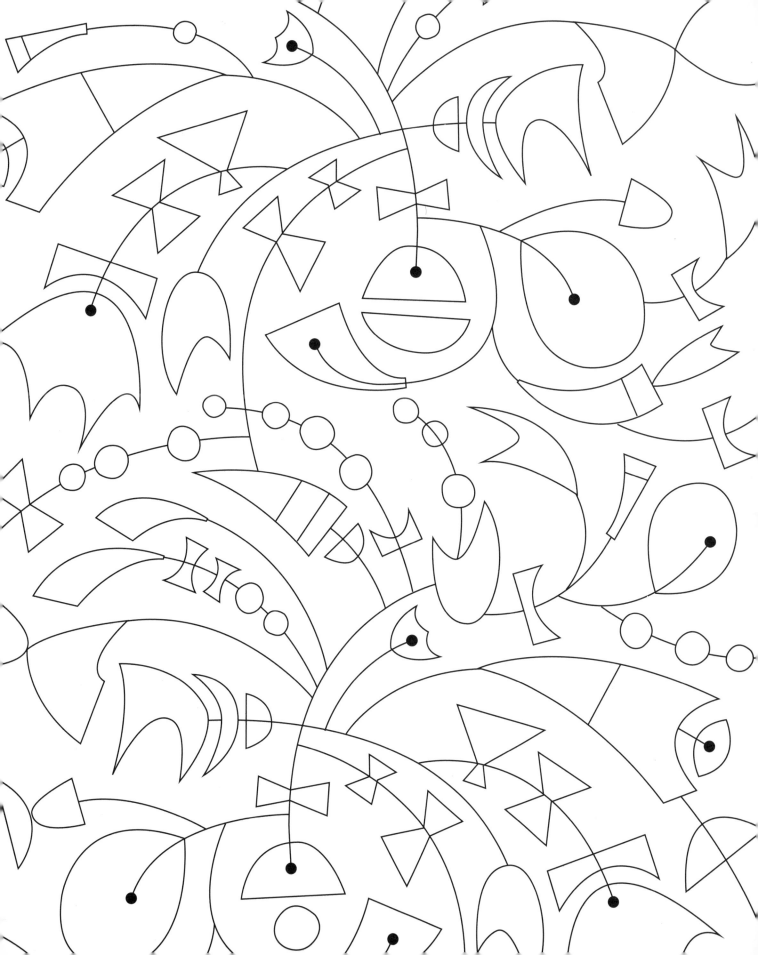

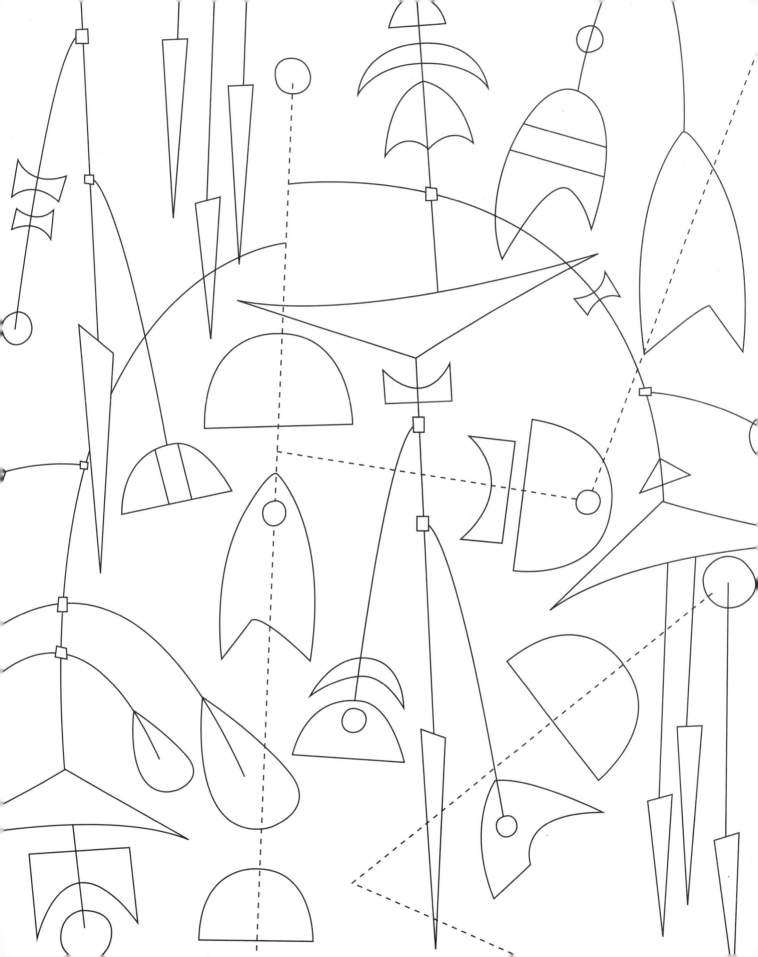

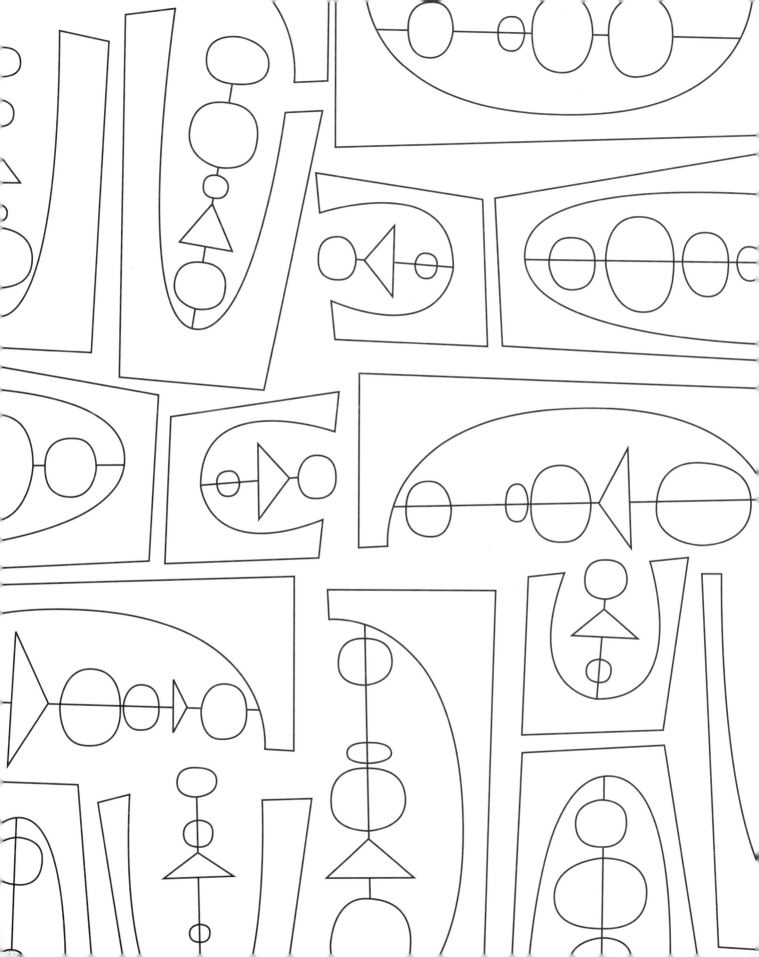

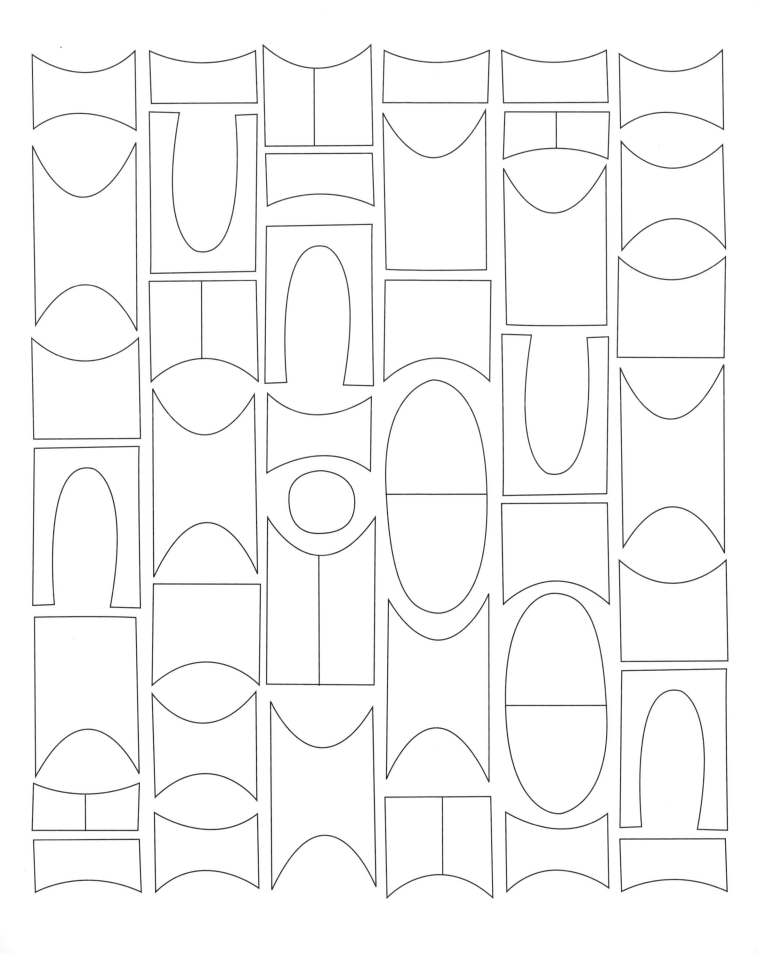

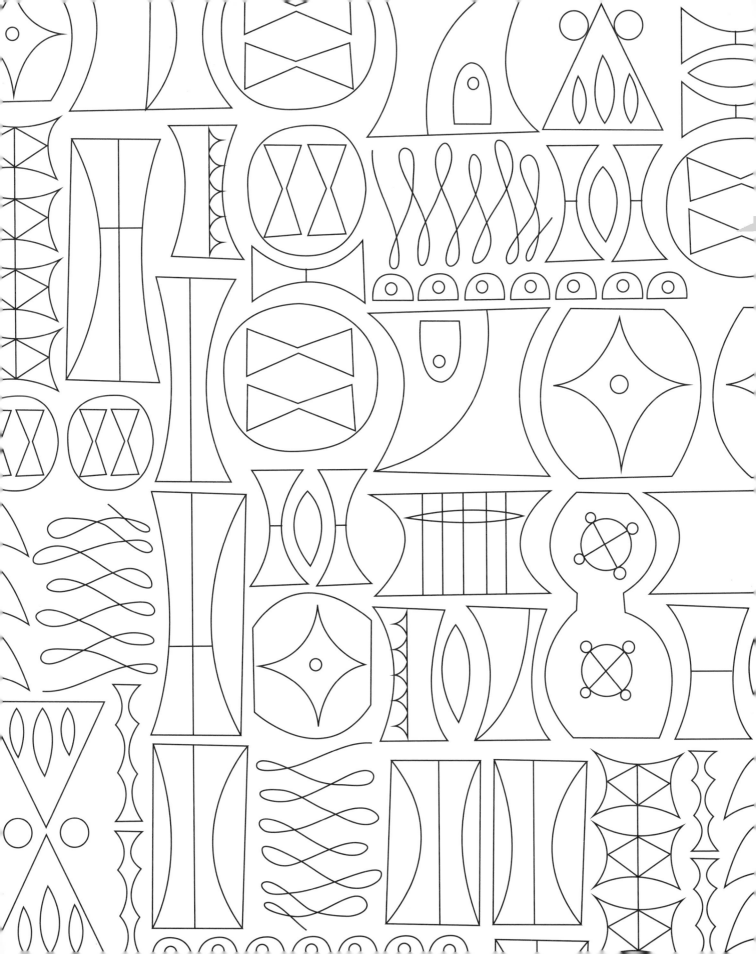

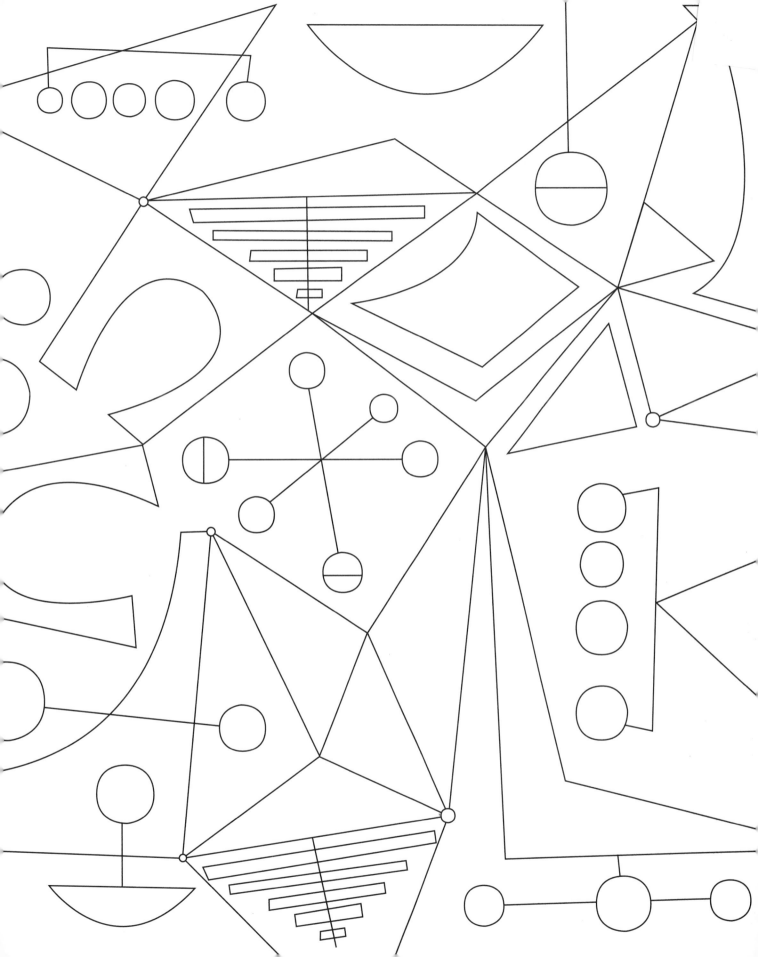

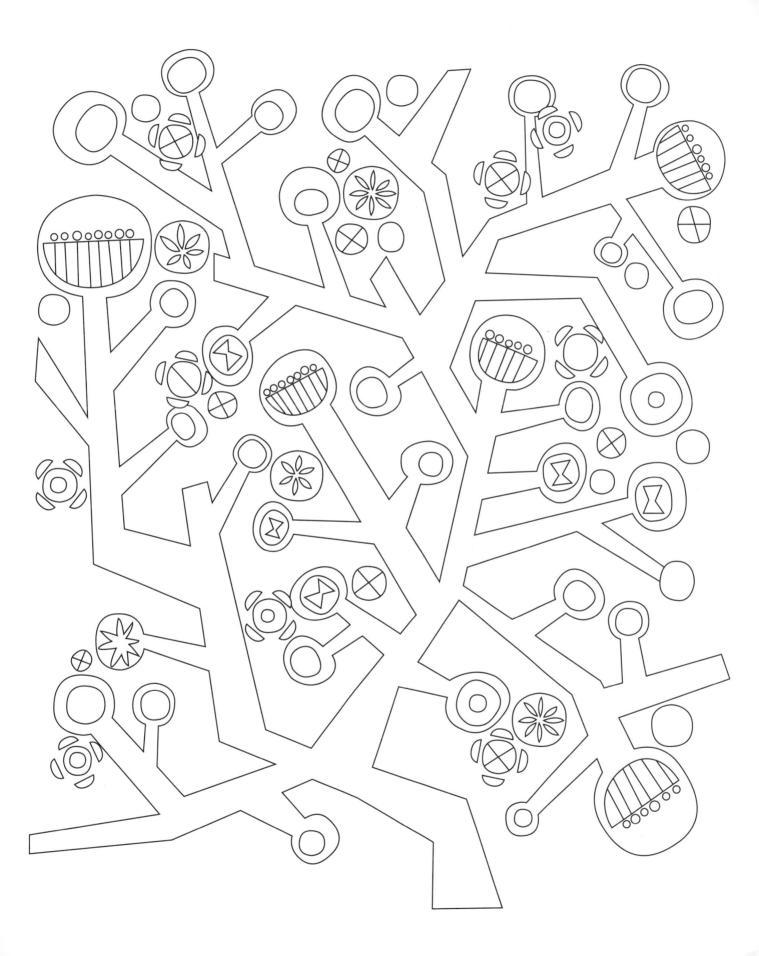

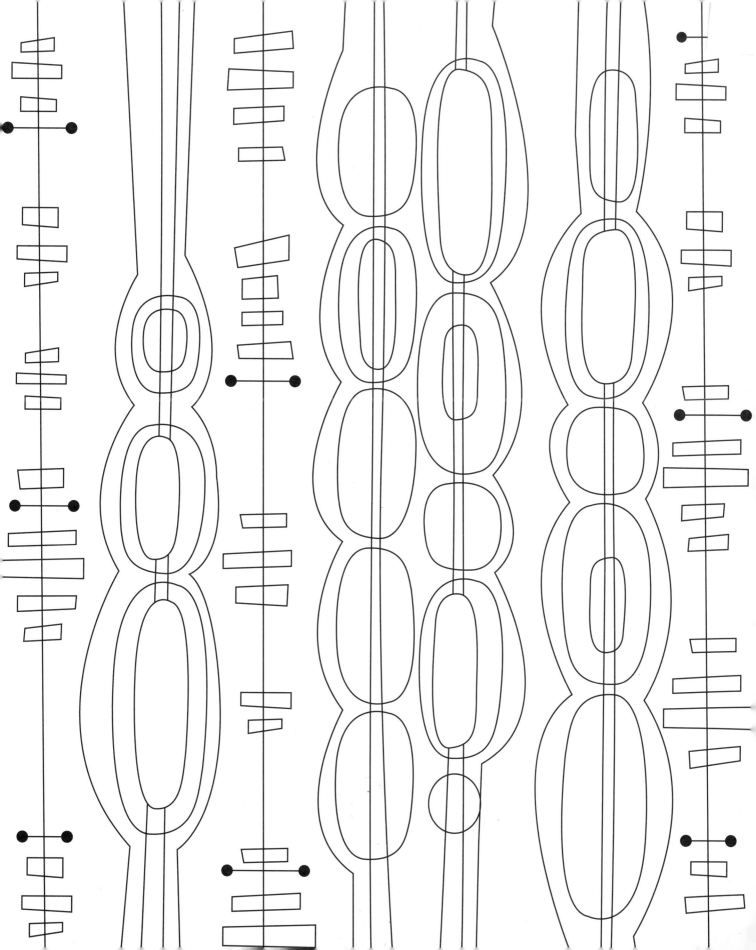

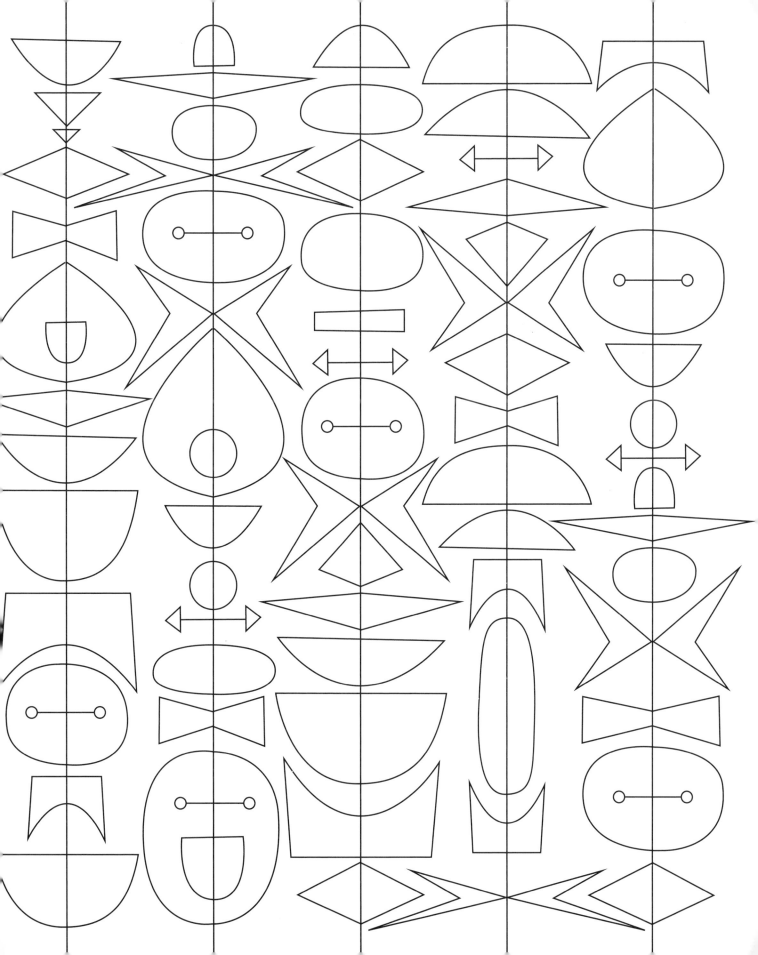

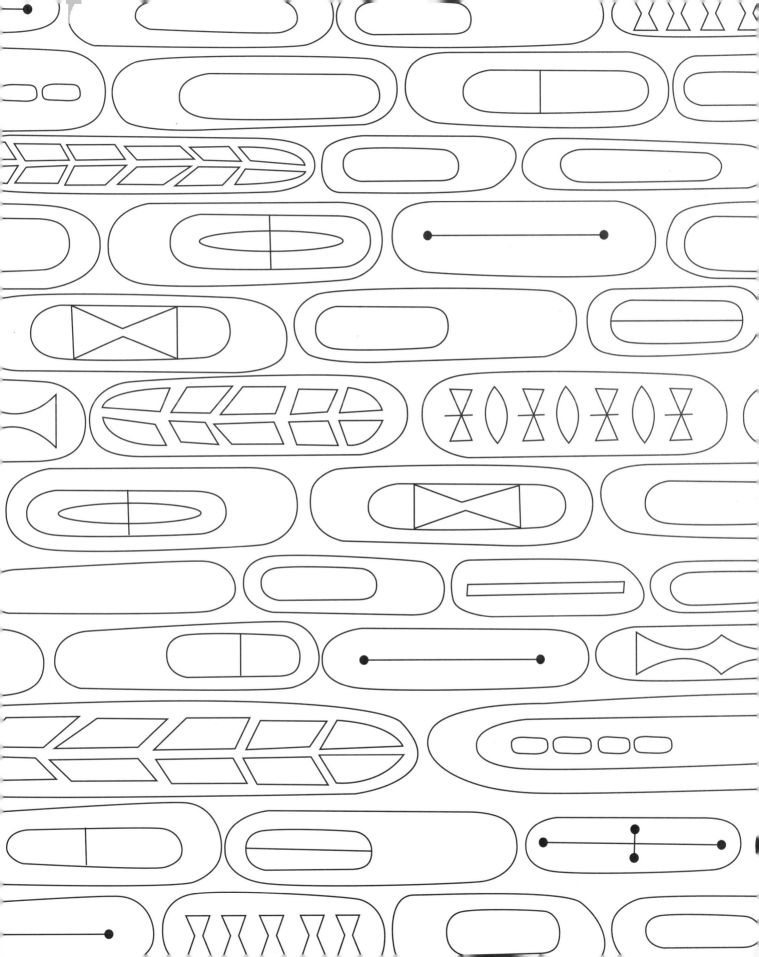

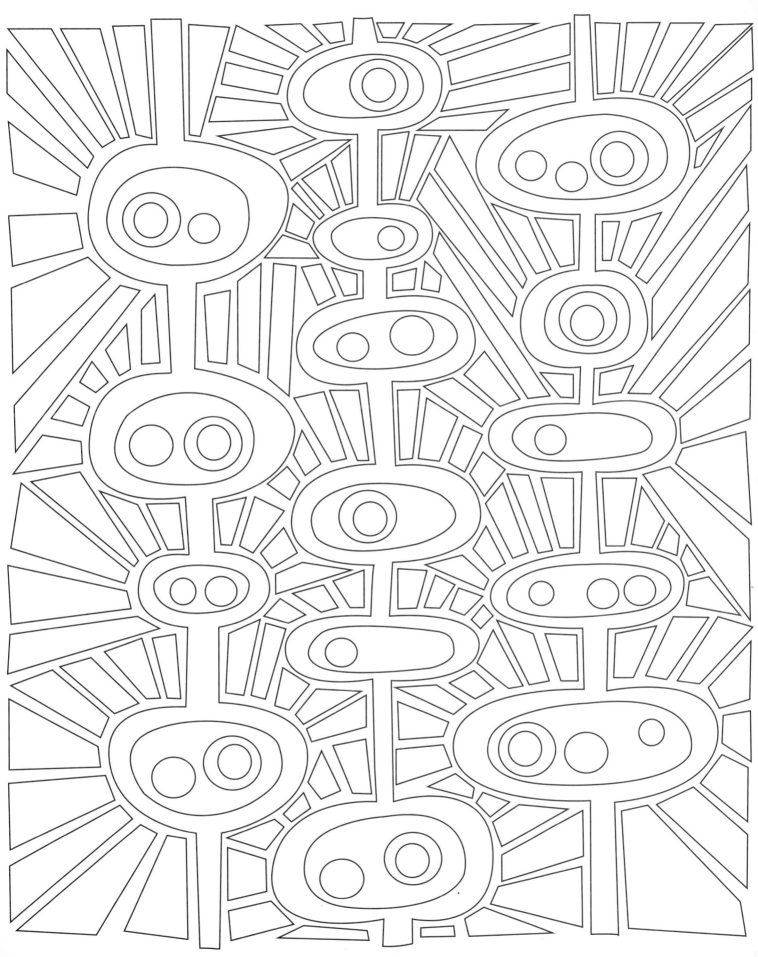

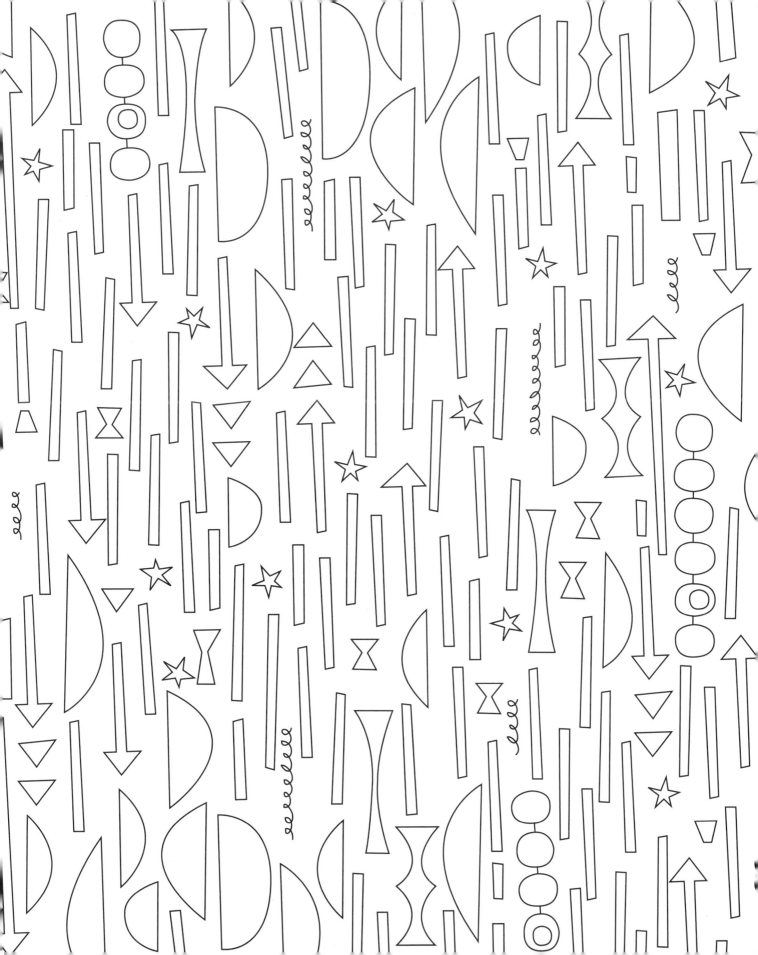

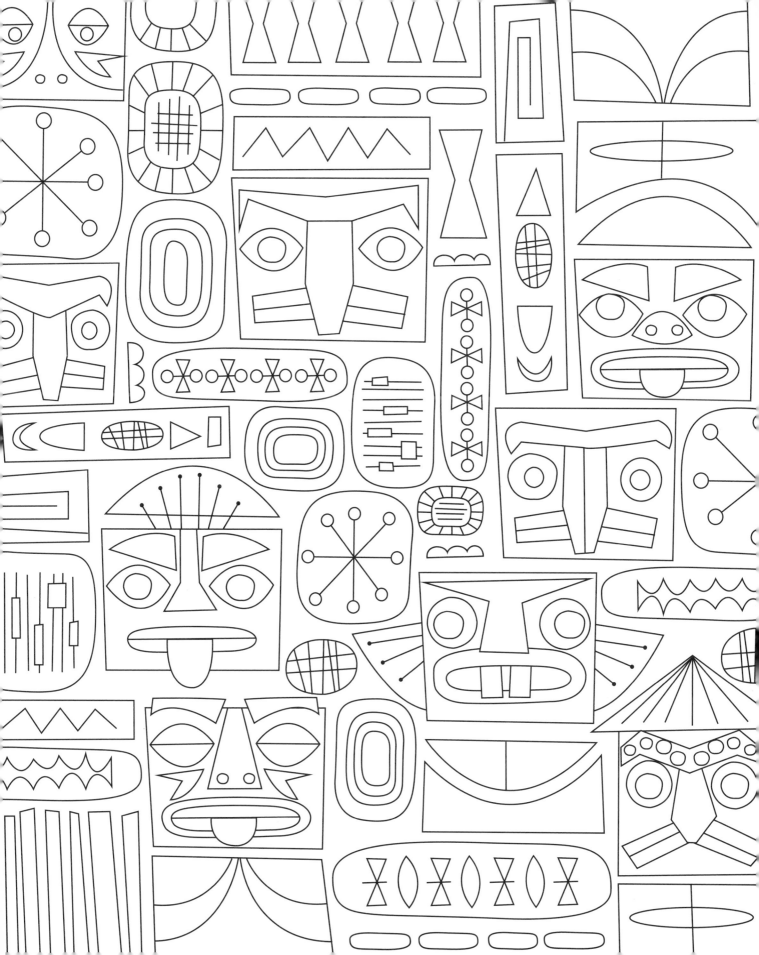

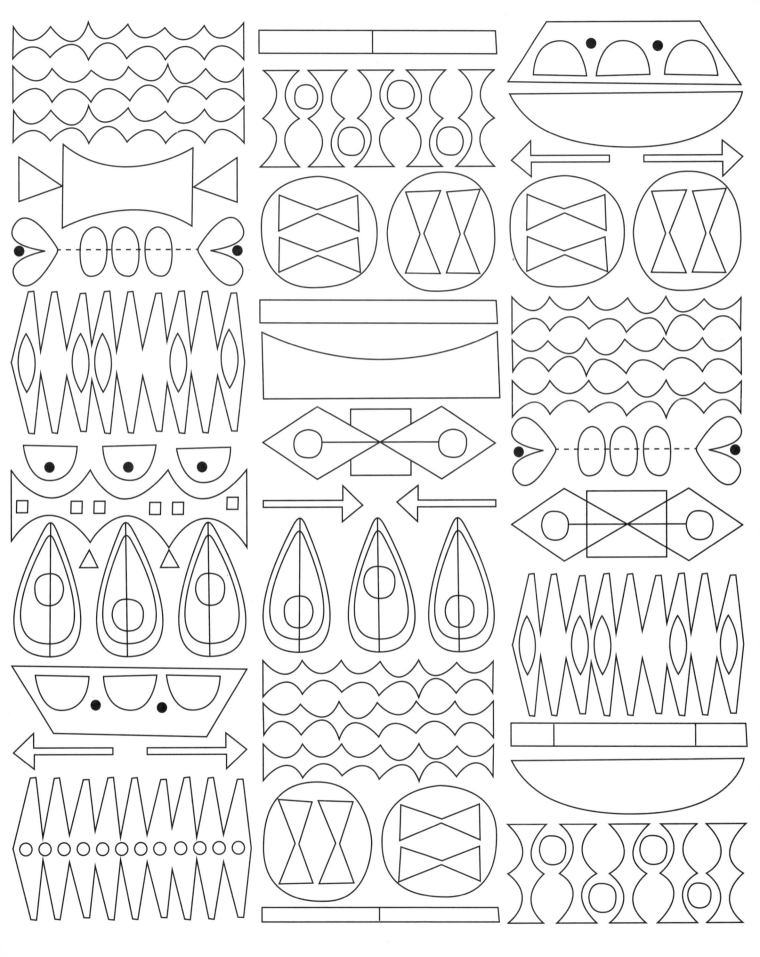

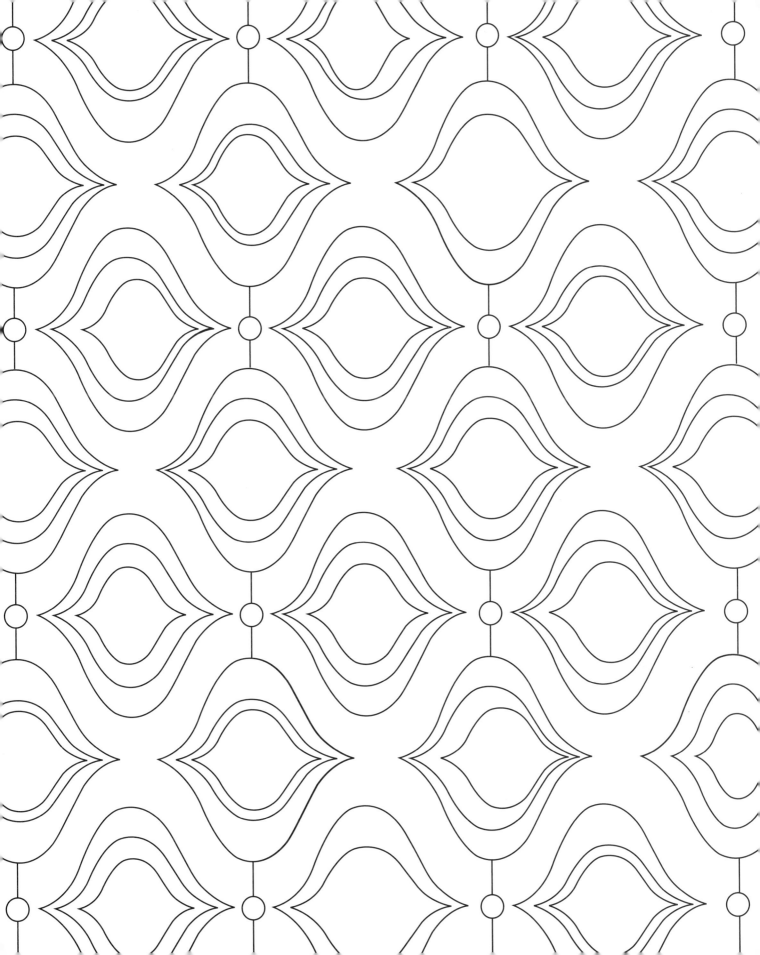

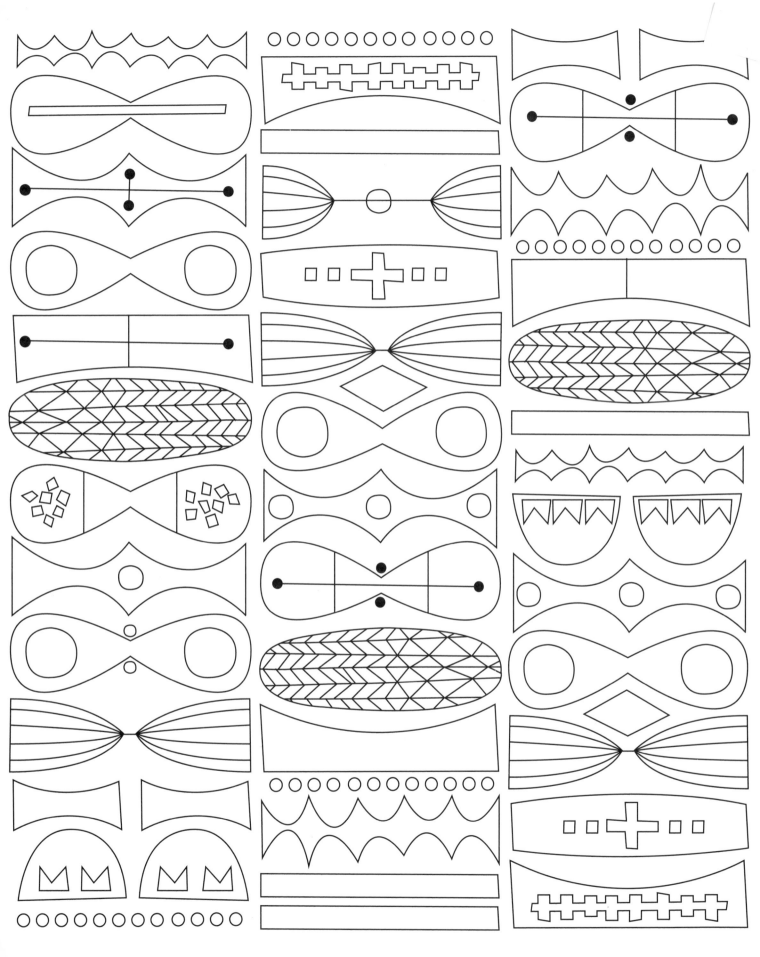

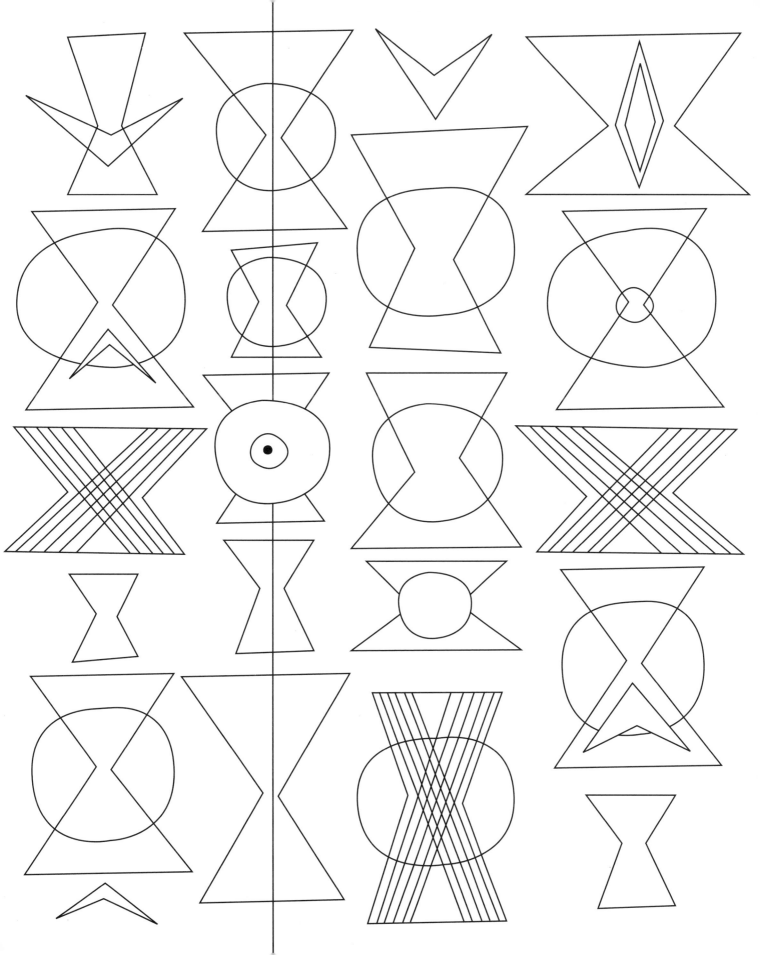

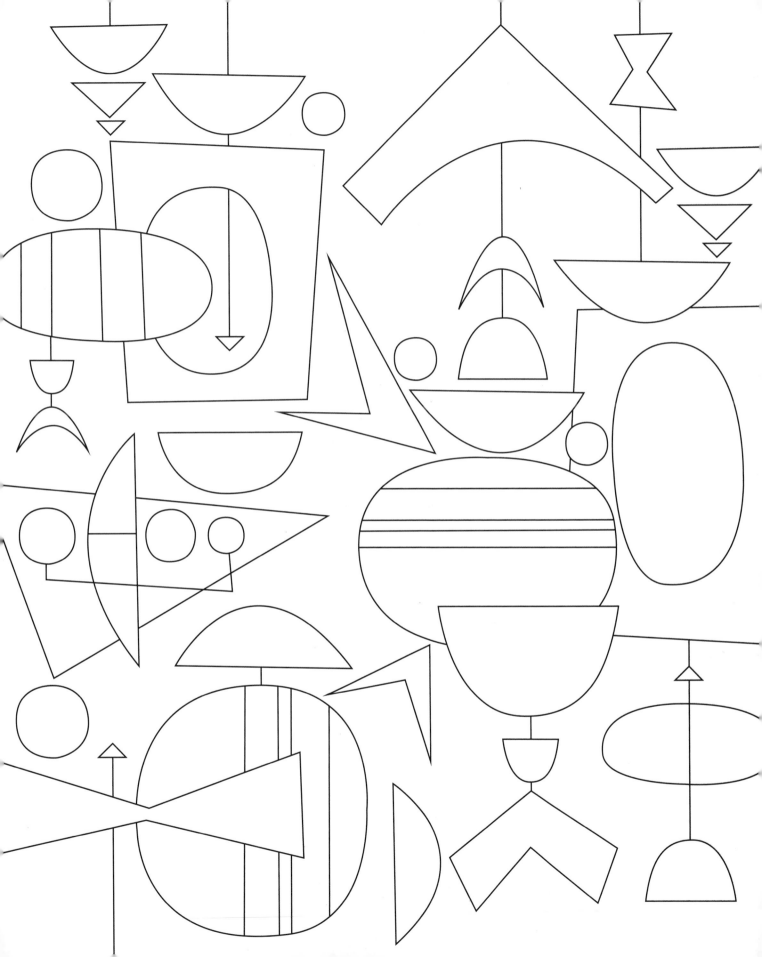

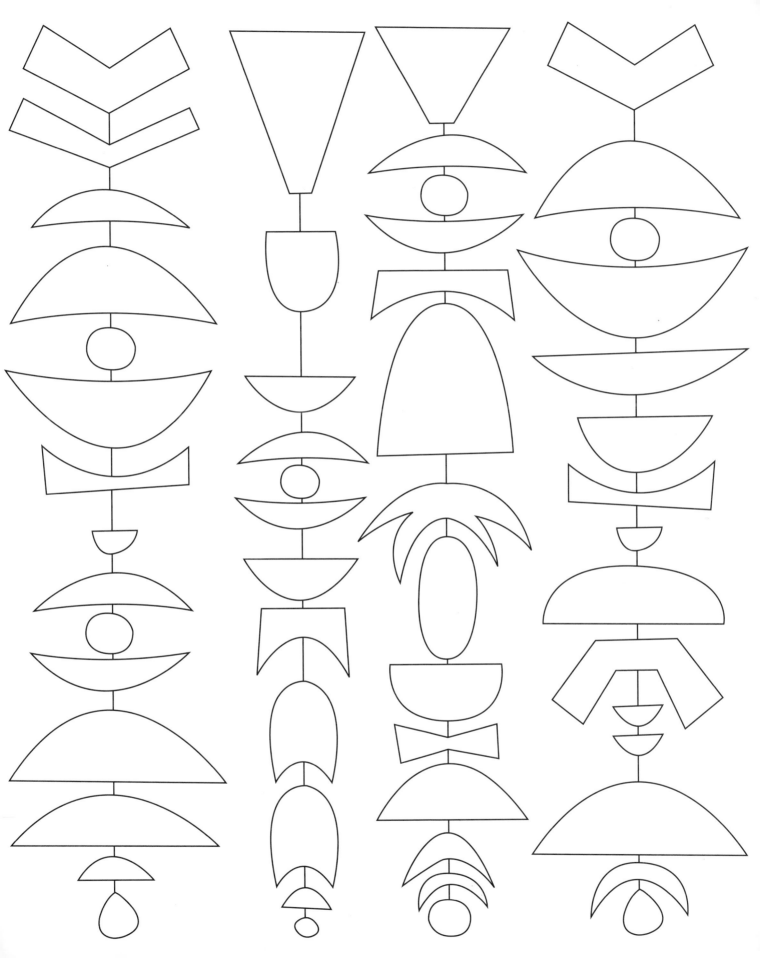

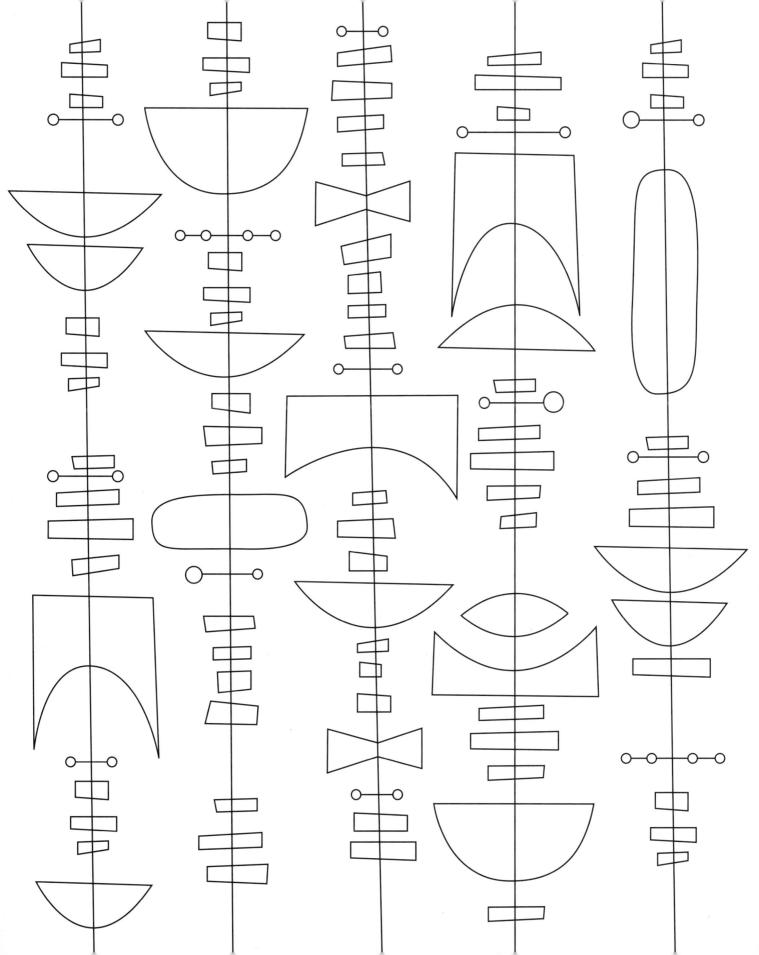

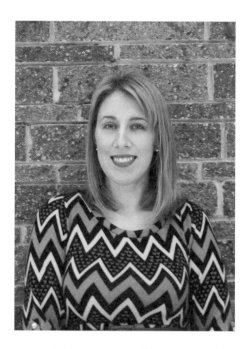

JENN SKI is an artist and illustrator with a passion for modern and mid-twentieth century art and design. She holds a BFA in graphic design from the University of Massachusetts, and her illustrations have been featured in countless publications and products, both in the United States and abroad. Jenn lives in Bedford, New Hampshire, with her husband, Al, and their cat, Floyd.

© 2014 Rockport Publishers
All images © 2014 Jenn Ski

First published in the United States of America
in 2014 by
Rockport Publishers, a member of
Quarto Publishing Group USA Inc.
100 Cummings Center
Suite 406-L
Beverly, Massachusetts 01915-6101
Telephone: (978) 282-9590
Fax: (978) 283-2742
www.rockpub.com
Visit RockPaperInk.com to share your opinions,
creations, and passion for design.

10 9 8 7

ISBN: 978-1-59253-946-8

Cover and Interior Design: Debbie Berne
Cover Image: Jenn Ski

Printed in China